BUSINESS

—— IS ——

WAR

BUSINESS

—— IS ——

WAR

Tactics for a Winning Strategy

ELLIOTT FORMAN

Dedication

Dedicated to my mother, you are the perfect example of love. I appreciate you and treasure you.

Acknowledgements

This book would not be possible without my loving wife, Porsche. To my family and friends who have been steadfast in their love and support, I thank you from the bottom of my heart.

To my Bonita family, we are partners until the end.

To my boxing family, we know each other in ways that go beyond traditional friendships. We know each other as brothers and sisters in arms. Our bond is above question, and I will always rely on you to reset me when my suit and tie don't fit like the gloves once did.

To business owners worldwide, I salute you. I know your challenges and wish to encourage you to keep going and never give up. Accepting that business is at war is the start of growing past its pains. Keep innovating, keep pushing, keep grinding. You are the difference makers.

CONTENTS

Introduction

Starting a business is not for the weak. Business Is War™. With the right mindset and better tools, you can win this war. I have filled this book with information on how to start, grow, and scale your business. Inside, we talk about the business landscape and the battles you'll encounter while running your business. You'll discover what it takes to achieve everything you want—plus more.

In today's world, casually approaching how to start and scale a business isn't going to cut it. The coffee shop owner is competing with major chains that can produce things quicker and cheaper. The local steakhouse has to do much more than just sourcing the meat and cooking the steak to keep people coming in the door.

Every detail counts. Every moment counts. Getting tough, understanding the business world, and challenging the fears that hold most business owners back will help guide you to success. In this book, I'm sharing the tools and techniques I've used with countless clients to help them move their businesses from surviving to thriving.

Pugilism [noun]-- the art, practice, or profession of fighting with the fist: boxing.

In The Ring

There is nothing harder than being a Boxer. Boxing is referred to as the loneliest sport, and it is by far just that. Sure, some sports require tremendous physical skills that only the smallest percentage of people have. Still, when it comes to mental anguish, constant internal battles, and suffering, boxing is the pinnacle of operating in pain.

There is something special and chosen about those who are called to put on the gloves. These people are God's poor children; they need all the support they can get. Boxing is the most work and the lowest reward, as in the unhealthiest relationships.

I have jumped more rope, punched more bags, and run more miles, all with no end in sight. I've starved myself for weeks at a time and suffered in silence while others ran through the years of life in a much more rewarding fashion. I missed parties and birthdays and lost more relationships than I care to remember. There is a good bit of my life that I don't remember because I was in the ring, both in my mind and my body.

The fight doesn't just start when the bell rings; it is in every day and every hour of your existence. Boxing is all about delaying gratification. It is the journey of sacrifice that only the most broken people will ever try to walk. And only those who have ever been on this path can understand how much I cannot describe in writing.

Survival, understanding the true essence of time, and trying to gather some level of pride in one's existence all go out of the window when the ringing of the bell becomes your beacon.

Boxing is the most self-inflicted life that anyone could ever willingly choose. No level of rationale can make you want to get punched in the face for money. No level of intelligence would have you risk the enormous damage from losing in front of the world, all for the chance to win and raise your hands in victory.

This Is Your Beacon

Running a business is just like boxing. It's a fight for survival, and it takes extreme sacrifice to succeed. Once you understand the Battles Of Business™ and how to prepare your business for taxes, capital, and human resources, you'll build a stronger future for your business, your family, and yourself.

With a healthier business, you secure a better future for everyone around you. Your employees, family, and everyone else will benefit from your efforts. One intelligent, healthy business can rewrite the destiny of your bloodline.

If you ignore the Battles of Business™ I lay out in this book, those battles will eat at your edges until they consume you. You risk never growing and fighting the uphill battle for survival. You risk losing more than your business, and you risk losing your time.

Are you ready to enter the ring and reach your full potential as a business owner? Then, allow me to show you what's stopping you from having a thriving business and how you can win every round in your fight.

Chapter 1

Fear Of The Unknown

"Success is not final, failure is not fatal;
it is the courage to continue that counts."
~ Winston Churchill

One of these thoughts is probably going through your head right now:

"I have a great idea but don't know where to start."

"I've started a business and don't know what's next."

"Maybe I should just close the doors."

"We are open but not making any money."

You're stuck because you don't have the information you need to help you move forward. The business world is a battlefield full of landmines that will kill your dreams. The number one rule in boxing is to "protect yourself at all times." Make one wrong move, and you're finished. Stay in place, and your opponent will catch you with your hands down.

Fear of the Jump

How long have you been thinking of launching your business? What's holding you back?

You know you have a great vision but don't know how to monetize it. The unknown factors leave you feeling lost about where to begin. You're probably asking, "Should I form the business first?"

Or, you already formed the business before you picked up this book. You've been running it for a while and are now stuck. The battles are stacking up, and you feel like you're losing, but you don't know what to do next.

Either way, you are ready to absorb the knowledge to help you make that jump. You're on the hunt for the answers to your most pressing questions.

Don't do too much too soon.

So many people start the meter running before they actually make money, and this starts the uphill climb at the beginning of their journey. Spending too much money before you make any money is what I call self-destruction. When you start your business, you want to play offense and defense equally. If you start the meter with no revenue, you will undoubtedly play defense and climb uphill from that point forward.

We started Bonita Payments with internet cables in the trunk of my Volkswagen and a couple of credit card machines. We drove our office around, supporting hundreds of clients for years before upgrading to a company vehicle. My first employee would meet me at a centrally located Starbucks, and we would start our day there. We got an actual office location eight years after earning revenues and were embarrassed about not doing it sooner. We started the meter when we had revenue and justification for the growth. This path is like the food truck to a brick-and-mortar graduation pace.

Tapering our growth until the business deserved the reward became the main reason we did not fail. If you've done too much too soon with your business, now is the time to reassess everything and fortify your foundation. Grow when you've made your business ready to handle the growth. Improving your business is a lifelong journey that requires subtle adjustments on a regular basis. As Apple's iPhone would call it: software updates.

Protecting The Perimeter

Let's say you made it through the first year, but the market has changed. Your revenues just took a dive, and now you're in a place where many businesses fail—where most do not know how to pivot for survival.

You need more capital. You have to do whatever it takes to keep the doors open so that you can keep doing what you want to do. Are you obsessed with keeping the doors open? Are you going to stick it out? Successful companies must master pivoting to thrive and grow.

Your business is not thriving, and you fear losing it altogether. You need a "road map" to success that will scale your company to the next level. You're ready to wage the war against the forces threatening your business.

Your survival rate dramatically drops if you don't gear up with the ammunition you need. Statistically, 18% of small businesses fail within their first year. You may have made it beyond year one, but you still have plenty of battles. We know that 50% fail after five years, and nearly 65% fail by their tenth year.[1]

Never Go Into Combat Alone

You need a partner who will watch your back. Running a business can be a lonely place to be without support. Being the best at what you do doesn't mean you're the best at everything, including running a business. You don't know what you don't know, which should scare you.

We can help you achieve a master's level in all aspects of business and show you how getting support through it will help you achieve your goals. With a wealth of knowledge, a support system, and conversations with other business owners and coaches, we'll help you navigate the landmines that make many businesses fail.

It starts here. This book will introduce you to the Business of War™ and the 12 battles you face. We'll give you the ammunition to attack whatever comes your way. By the end, you'll be ready to take the steps you need to master all aspects of your business.

---

[1] Chamber of Commerce Team. (2024, April 12). *Small business statistics*. Chamber Of Commerce. https://www.chamberofcommerce.org/small-business-statistics/

Chapter 2

Business Is War™

"Let your plans be dark and impenetrable as night. And
when you move, fall like a thunderbolt."

~ Sun Tzu

> **WAR -**
>
> noun. A conflict carried on by force of arms, as between nations or
> between parties within a nation; warfare, as by land, sea, or air. A
> state or period of armed hostility or active military operations: The
> two nations were at war with each other.

Nothing about the business environment is fair, equitable,
inclusive, or friendly. One minute, you're happy. The next minute,
you're in the dumps. Business Is War™. It's not personal. It's
business. It must thrive and grow to survive. It has to be ready for
the what-ifs and the challenges you cannot see yet.

Lies, Deception, and Sneak Attacks

When a guy robs you, he sticks a pistol in your face. You get to see the weapon and understand the importance of your next move. In business, there are no guarantees. People pencil-whip you and rob you far worse than the villain with a gun. It happens every day. The finance manager at the dealership has you approved for five percent but writes the paperwork at eight; that is business. So many people fall victim to the decimal in the world of finance. The discrimination tax is when the real estate agent charges you more than a different prospective tenant. The discrimination tax is a landmine on the real estate battleground that far too many have fallen victim to.

In business, a lot of nasty stuff happens between guys with degrees who wear suits and ties. I had to get into corporate America to understand that the only thing they're doing is controlling money. It's about money, power, and greed. It happens in ways you likely cannot see. I will never understand why someone making money will sabotage the next man trying to earn a living.

I know for a fact that corporations will surround the little guys and just starve them into failure. They suffocate the competition —this happens every day. At least the thug is going to show you the gun. Corporate America will smile, and they use their Montblanc™ ink pens and cut your business in half.

Who is more criminal—the thug with the pistol or the suit and tie with his fancy fountain pen? One uses fear, and the other uses power. They are both strategies of war.

The business battleground is nastier and sneakier. Look at how often someone in history told someone else an idea, only to see it on the television the next day. It's a race to see who can get it out first and move the crowd to make the most money.

Only one in ten startup businesses ultimately survive. That means 90% of all startups will eventually fail. Business Is War™. If you do not want to become one of the 90%, you must understand the battles you have to fight to maintain success.[2]

If you are the best at what you do and obsessed with success, you're in the right place. You've got what it takes to thrive and grow, no matter what gets thrown at you! Just look at what you will get inside this book.

Battles of Business™ for Success

I've divided these Battles of Business™ into 12 battlegrounds. During any of these battles, an enemy can sneak up behind you and attack. When you master these areas of your business, you're ready for the what-ifs and environmental changes that affect your business.

Battle #1: Craftsmanship.
In Chapter 3: Master Your Craft, I discuss how to break down what you are a master at, how it fits within the market, and why it is your "secret weapon" that sets you above the rest on the battleground.

---

[2] Howarth, J. (2023, November 3). *Startup failure rate statistics (2024)*. Exploding Topics. https://explodingtopics.com/blog/startup-failure-stats

Battle #2: Feelings.

In chapter four, we look at the feelings your business produces, the experiences your clients or customers desire, and how to monetize that.

Battle #3: Mission.

In chapter five, I go through why having your mission from the start will help drive your business forward and how it's constantly evolving, not just a done-once statement.

Battle #4: Scalability.

In chapter six, I'll help you understand how transforming the massive support model to scalable will increase your revenue.

Battle #5: Numbers.

In chapter seven, I'll take you through one of the areas that sink many business owners—understanding the cost of goods sold and the market.

Battle #6: Real Estate.

In chapter eight, we examine one of your business's most intense battles and how you can gear up for optimal growth and success.

Battle #7: Sales.

In chapter nine, we look at sales and why mastering this is critical to your business's survival.

Battle #8: Marketing.

In chapter ten, I'll help you avoid one of the biggest mistakes failed businesses make: failing to align their marketing with their sales.

Battle #9: Human Resources.
In chapter eleven, we examine one of the most challenging battles to handle because you cannot control the variables. Don't worry— you can still win this battle!

Battle #10 Taxes.
In chapter twelve, we examine how to simplify the process of shifting from a W-2 employee mindset to a business mindset during one of the most frustrating battles business owners face.

Battle #11: Capital.
In chapter thirteen, we emphasize how critical it is to your business success that you know and understand how to use money as a tool.

Battle #12: Mindset.
In chapter fourteen, we dispel many common misconceptions about the successful business owner's mindset about work, life, and business.

This Book Is Not For You If...

If any of these are true for you, this is probably not the book you want to read.

- You want to do as little as possible and get a check.
- You are satisfied with the status quo.
- You are okay with failure.
- You are a talker but not a doer.
- You are not obsessed with conquering your world.

If any of the above is you, it is okay to put this book down and go on with your life. It's okay if you want to say, "This is bullshit. No!" I will not hold you back.

What Makes This Book Right For You:

If you can say, "Yes! That's me," to any of the below, this book is for you.

- You're a growth-minded person looking for an opportunity.
- You're stuck in a job with enough money to start something but just don't know where to begin.
- You're ready to go up one more level on the ladder.
- You want more than you're getting right now and are looking for guidance on making that happen.
- You're a small business owner struggling to get unstuck or struggling to elevate your revenue.

Let me tell you a little bit about myself. After serving in the military, I moved back to New Orleans, where I became a professional boxer. I always had an aptitude for technology and got into technology sales. Then, I transitioned into fintech sales and aggressively climbed the corporate ladder.

I spent ten years in corporate America before transitioning into entrepreneurship and building my company. That was ten years ago, so I'm writing this book with more than 20 years of experience in fintech sales and ten years of experience in company leadership. We've made money every year, and I've genuinely thought about it, down to every penny, every day.

The Business Is War™ Mindset

My time in the military and as a professional boxer has formed my mindset regarding business: simply put, kill or be killed. My single most significant takeaway from the Military is to train and operate in readiness for battle. My biggest takeaway from professional Boxing was to put in the reps. Every single day is an opportunity to develop, sharpen, and master your craft.

I trained in boxing for fights that never happened. I worked out for an opponent who was better than me, more skilled than me, and better prepared than I was. That person was the man in the mirror. I would never meet this fighter because my imagination kept pushing him further and further away from me. My training was self-destructive because my mind never let me feel ready for the fight. This thinking resulted in a morbid existence marred with misery and self-doubt.

Fear is the central operating policy for a fighter. Now that I look back, I don't even know exactly what I was afraid of. I became comfortable in this realm of isolation, and the more I trained, the more I believed that my opponent was training for me. This kept me going!

This paranoia is what makes me obsessed with preparing for the battle of business. Imagine if you went into combat and you were unprepared! That is not something that I can live with. I told myself the day of the fight that I would die rather than not try my hardest. I feared not doing my best more than the man that was across the ring gloved up to kill me. I learned to trick myself into thinking more about the date of the fight than the opponent. The closer the date got, the less the man became relevant.

If you plan on starting a business and you are not all in, do yourself and your loved ones a favor —**don't!** It makes no sense to start a marathon and not finish—there is no lesson in that. You would do better to train for a marathon and not run one. You could salvage the benefit of being in shape and living the lifestyle of a runner.

If you think business is easy, simply read the Yelp reviews of the closest businesses to your house. Put yourself into the business owner's shoes and see how the public views them. Imagine pouring your heart into a recipe and a customer tells everyone that the food sucks because they don't like, let's say, pasta—this is a real-life situation that happens every day.

Business is WAR™. It is very personal and should be treated with care and handled accordingly. A poorly run and trashy business means some owner is not all in, and the product is the proof!

I will show you how to develop a bulletproof business that thrives and grows with the times. Forget your fears about AI. Forget your fears about big business squeezing you out. Forget about the recession. You're here to win!

Chapter 3

Master Your Craft

"Your job is to build something that users love."

~ Sam Altman

What are you a master at?

Sometimes, the answer is clear, such as having a desire and aptitude for shoe repair, and you know you want to open a shoe repair business. Sometimes, it's not so clear, but you know you have a mastery of something. In this case, you will need to do some soul-searching and determine what product or service you will offer.

What do you enjoy doing, and what are you good at doing? The combination of these things will show you what you're uniquely a master of. This is where you'll have mastery and success.

"A jack of all trades is a master of none, but oftentimes better than a master of one."

~ quote used to describe William Shakespeare

It's not always just one thing. It could be a combination of things that make you a master. If you're good at sales and understand tech, your mastery might be selling tech, which gives you the unique ability to scale tech.

Creating Your Combined Skill Set

Sometimes, your mastery is that your idea is so good that you just have to monetize it, period. And you've got a head start because you've done the detailed mental aspect of this particular level of craftsmanship.

For instance, technology embodies both craftsmanship and mastery. Proprietary information represents a form of mastery and shows how mastery doesn't always have to be a tangible skill. It can also be a strategic innovation. For example, at one point in history, a forward-minded thinker said, "Let's develop LCD televisions because everyone else is using projector tube models that just don't match the quality of our sets." This innovative idea, rooted in craftsmanship and mastery, was successfully monetized.

Your concept, your tech, your idea, and your ingenuity are so good that you can put it into the market in a replicable fashion. Think back to before forklifts were invented. Moving warehouse inventory was strenuous and dangerous, and it slowed warehouses down. That presented a problem, limiting our supply chain efficiency. Invent the forklift, replicate them, and sell them...problem solved. Warehouse workflow improved, leading to better pallet designs that helped fuel the need for more forklifts across industries. [3]

---

[3] Steel, A. S. (2023, December 21). *Forklift history: Unravel the astonishing evolution of power.* Equip Insights. https://equipinsights.com/forklift-history-evolution

Your combined skills need to solve a big enough problem in a unique way that encourages a demand for it. The better your idea, the less you have to explain it. Sometimes your idea is so good that you have to start it!

Two ways to make money:

1→ Buy low and sell high in the retail world.

2→ Provide a service at an exceptionally proficient rate and charge for it.

Develop Your Mastery

"It takes 10,000 hours of intensive practice to achieve mastery of complex skills and materials."

~ Malcolm Gladwell in Outliers

Mastering your craft means being obsessed with what it is that you do. You have to know every aspect of it. You have to be passionate about it. People looking for shortcuts don't reach mastery.

Follow this rule: If you're not great at it and you don't enjoy it, don't do it.

Look To The Future

If you have a family-owned business, planning this craftsmanship phase out for the future becomes critical. In 2nd and 3rd generation businesses, the parents are the masters of the craft. Then, when the company passes down, the work ethics and skill sets change.

There is no guarantee that the same level of craftsmanship and mastery will pass from generation to generation. How many family businesses survive the transition from first-generation to second? 30 percent. Only 12% survive the transition from 2nd to 3rd generation.[4] In case you're wondering about the 4th generation, less than 4% survive.

Mastery Isn't Enough

Congratulations! You have some clarity on what you are a master of, but guess what? You can still fail. The battleground of craftsmanship is full of landmines.

You may be bringing out your idea before people are ready for it. Think back to when Blu-ray Discs came out. They were so expensive no one wanted to pay $70 for them when the VHS was only $3.50. To survive, they had to reduce manufacturing costs to reproduce them at a price people were willing to pay.

You may not be able to reproduce your idea in a timely and cost-effective manner where it makes sense to keep moving forward. We'll discuss this more in chapter six.

You may fail to account for changes in your industry that affect your ability to get sales. For instance, no matter how good you are at washing cars, the drive-thru $7 car wash has strongly impacted that industry. And I know this because I used to have clients with highly successful auto detail shops.

---

[4] SCORE (2023, June 28) SCORE.ORG, SCORE, accessed 22 March 2024, Infographic: The Family Business—Successes and Obstacles https://www.score.org/resource/infographic/infographic-family-business%E2%80%94successes-and-obstacles.

There was this guy we'll name John. John used to hand wash cars, and he could service 40 cars a day with help. He is now out of business because the local automated car wash lets you drive through with free vacuums in 90 seconds.

Is what you're offering desirable today? Remember that demand drives ingenuity. Think about how music with the Napster download brought us from 56k dial-up to high-speed broadband. People's desire to download music is the core reason we developed broadband. We wanted to stream it better without the infuriating 5-hour wait.

Take a close look at your idea. Is it powerful enough to overcome any of these problems? If not, what needs to happen to make your idea successful?

What Makes You Unique?

USP stands for Unique Selling Proposition, and it is what differentiates your offering from everyone else's. It's the customizations of your craftsmanship. Anyone can cut hair, but can you provide a location and consistent results that people love? Anyone can bake a cake, but can you package that cake and do it consistently enough to build your fanfare?

Craftsmanship is one thing, but you have to upscale your presentation skills. How do you make your offering different, and how do you do that consistently? How can your business be unique in your industry?

If you cook the best steak in the area, how many will buy it if you serve it on a paper plate? You need to learn presentation skills to create a sensation at the table. What comes with that steak? What's in your package (sides, vegetables, dessert)? It's like how that Gucci belt must come in a phenomenal box, not a brown paper bag. Packaging has a significant impact here.

I'll discuss this more in the upcoming chapters, starting with the client experience in chapter 4.

Chapter 4

What Is It Like To Do Business With You?

The best way to control your customer experience
is to intentionally create it.
~ Elle Robertson

What Feeling Does Your Business Give?

You're on the Feeling Battleground now. Take a second to think about a business that left a positive, lasting impression on you. What made it memorable, and why did it resonate with you? I bet it's because they did a lot of things right, plus extras on top of that. You likely shared that experience with someone because it made a powerful impression on you.

More business owners should be wondering what their client experience looks like. Maybe you cook great food at your restaurant, but how do the people feel when they leave? How do they feel while they are there? Not enough business owners ask, "What is it like to do business with me?" and put a real onus on crafting that experience and how that feeling looks. Yeah, the food was good, but what about everything else?

No Birds, No Problem

What makes Disney World better than everywhere else? Disney thinks about the senses in customer experience better than anybody else. The smells, the music, the lack of birds...

What's with the birds? Nobody wanted them. Nobody wanted the mess, and nobody wanted the birdlife stealing their food while they ate. Disney built an entire system designed to deal with this problem, with a meticulous clean-up routine that eliminates trash on the ground that may attract them. The rides naturally discourage birds, plus Disney will play specific bird sounds through the speakers that help keep them away. That's why you may hear birds yet not see them.

Disney uses its mastery of the customer experience to build one of the happiest places on Earth.

Clean Under The Hood

Nothing will positively impact your business like cleaning it up. This maintenance gives you an in-depth look at your business. I have a saying—"If you don't know what to do, then clean." This nurturing can include everything from tax planning to marketing, designing ads, research, and other things to help you better understand your State of the Union. Most people don't know where the holes are because they're too busy paying attention to the loudest problem in the room. Do you know how many kitchens need attention? Do you know how many restaurant bathrooms would fail an inspection? Most businesses suffering from any number of battles can solve many of their problems by deep cleaning and looking under the hood.

My Favorite Bar

Let me tell you about a bar I visit and why I keep going back. I go there because they literally know my name. They have the four Ps of selling: people, place, product, and price. They have people who know your name. They have a product that I use. They have a reasonable price for me, and they're located right. They have all the Ps in place, so people buy from them. The human element is solid with people who treat you respectfully. How do you compete against a website? Add the best parts of people and you've got a fighter's chance. I call this the Cheers effect. It's a place that establishes a trusted connection with the customer and gives them consistency, which is vital to longevity.

Who else?

Now, let's dive into some bigger brands that have created an amazing client experience. Think about the problems they solve and how they monetize those for long-term success with their customer experience.

Chick-fil-A

Chick-fil-A has done a great job of using robot-like operations to build a positive customer experience. Each employee is an extension of the training and the leadership. You can get your order timely and accurately by going inside or through the drive-thru. "My pleasure" is the salutation to every order done right.

Amazon

Amazon Prime allows you to order anything you want today, and it will arrive tomorrow. It doesn't matter if it's something as small as a light bulb or dog food. They've created the best e-commerce platform in the world and changed the human shopping experience. They used ingenuity to determine what was in the way for their customers and found a way to make it easier, faster, and more rewarding. They're so good at it that other companies are learning from them and trying to catch up. Within seconds, you can search for an item, find ten versions of it, pay for it, and double-click to ship to your address on file.

Apple

Apple doesn't just provide exceptional technology; it is also a lifestyle. They eliminated the need for users to call customer service by using the best self-training model in business history. How is it that they deploy millions of devices each year and don't train people how to use them? Customers grab and go and don't ask any questions. They power on, add the Wi-Fi, and pick a language. People become advanced users who are self-taught experts in all things Apple.

Look at how the iPhone became the best technology in the last several decades. It is a calculator, camera, flashlight, compass, piano teacher, medical app, voice recorder, emailer, and even document handler. It solves so many problems in one transportable product. Twenty years ago, these were all different devices; now, they are just one. Apple solved many problems and has great technology, as do other companies. Still, it created a user experience and brand recognition that makes people loyal to its business.

If you ever walk into an Apple store, they're always going to have a new device or that new color you crave available. By the time you get to your car, you've already signed into your iCloud and are ready to do whatever you need without disruption. They've spent enough time making a bulletproof product, and I often see people confidently running million-dollar businesses from the iPhone.

Steve Jobs is an excellent example of someone who understood mastery and obsession. He took his mastery to market and obsessed over it to build one of the best customer experiences in the world.

Constantly Innovating To Be On Top

When Steve Jobs built the first iMac, it lacked one thing: the ability to compete with PCs that allowed users to rip off their own music CDs. Instead of upgrading the iMac to catch up, he created an integrated system that rocked the industry. This marked the birth of iTunes, the iTunes store, and the iPod.[5]

---

[5] Isaacson, W. (2014, October 29). The real leadership lessons of Steve Jobs. Harvard Business Review. https://hbr.org/2012/04/the-real-leadership-lessons-of-steve-jobs

Understanding Your Client's Senses

How do you use technology to create a seamless experience for your customers? Is your user interface aligned with the people who represent your brand? I want you to feel the business with all five senses: taste, touch, smell, hearing, and sight. Those feelings must align with your mission and core values so that you represent yourself when you put the product out in the market.

Retail stores have long been playing with the senses. Let me walk you through some examples.

When you walk into Abercrombie and Fitch, they have a fragrance machine that makes you ask in a good way, "Oh, my God, what is that smell?" It's a smell that makes you feel good, provides such a fantastic, soft landing for you to go in, and helps you feel more relaxed about spending your money there. The smell of the new car is undoubtedly one of the triggers for closing the deal, regardless of price; you cannot compete with how euphoric it is that makes you feel.

Have you ever noticed how a jewelry store will have the brightest lights in the entire shopping mall? You can't see anything initially, but everything is gleaming and glistening because they want the diamond to shine. That jewelry will never shine on your person like in the store, but you only have to buy it once.

Casinos use all five senses like a master puppeteer; the party never stops inside. The ringing sound is addictive to the gambler, and the flashing lights will make the time fly by, so you have no idea how 30 minutes turned into 5 hours. Add free drinks with tons of fake reward points and buffet vouchers, free hotel stays, and you are all in.

Bars use peanuts, popcorn, and pretzels to keep you thirsty. You keep drinking because they're giving you salt. Movie theaters make sure you smell the popcorn as soon as you walk in the door so that you just have to buy it, and if you don't, the smell will make you regret it. That bucket of popcorn gives the business the best profit margins, and they integrate it right into the customer experience.

Your Unique Sensory Engagement

Think about your customer journey. How do they first engage with your business? What is the process they move through to spend money with your business? How can you improve this journey?

Could you engage their senses differently?

How do your competitors use the five senses to engage with their customers?

What is the norm in your industry, and what can you change to become memorable?

Step Into The Ring With Confidence

Let's say you're opening a high-end restaurant, and your customer has just walked in the door. Picture your business as the boxing ring, and every guest is a boxer stepping into it. Just as a boxer relies on their senses to read their opponent, as the owner, you must leverage the five senses to understand your customer enough to craft a memorable dining experience.

Picture your menu selection as your arsenal of punches—each menu item should hit with precision and impact and be full of flavor. Start by sight; your branding, from the sign outside to the visual ambiance inside, should captivate them like the anticipation leading up to the championship match. Next, consider sound; your greetings, music, and kitchen sounds (sizzling steak) should resonate like the cheering crowd. Then, there's touch; your service should be as smooth and precise as a boxer's footwork, ensuring your guest feels like a visiting winner. Taste and smell become your knockout blows when your dishes feature delicious flavors that leave them craving more with every bite. Just like a skilled boxer anticipates their opponent's moves, a successful business owner anticipates their customers' needs and desires, using all their senses to deliver a winning experience.

Bonus: You Can Charge More!

You own a restaurant, and you welcome that person to your sit-down establishment. Let them use your utensils, napkins, condiments, resources, electricity, and television. You have every right to say, "This is how much I need to earn on this particular plate," because you control all the dynamics. You also provide them with music, and you have terrific decor. The restaurant is clean and safe. A security guard stands outside, ensuring your patrons' safety. A valet parks their cars.

You may be offering the same steak that someone's cooking at their backyard BBQ and serving to others out of their garage, but your steak has more value. You have all five senses engaged in a high-end steakhouse where you create a truly memorable experience to go with that steak. You can tell them how much you want to charge, which justifies all those extras. And people will love paying that price.

Outsmart Your Opponent

Curating your customer's experience is crucial in determining your price points. Establishing your pricing strategy is much like stepping into the ring with a skilled veteran. A well-executed jab can manage the fight in the boxing ring. Understanding your offers and their perceived value is the first tool for setting the perfect price point.

Imagine that you're in the ring, sizing up your opponent. It's the same in the market. You need to know your rival's moves. What is the competition charging? How are they labeling their combos? If you're serving up a knockout burger but labeling it as just a "burger," you're giving a lackluster customer experience.

When you step into the ring of pricing strategies, you need more than just jabbing your opponent with a naming strategy. Agility and footwork help you determine optimal flexibility when it comes to pricing. What is in the most demand this season? What time of the day is the busiest? What customer segment is most attracted to your dish?

Don't forget to add combination punches to your fighting style. Bundling your knockout hamburger with complementary items like your signature fries and a drink creates a value perception that justifies a higher price point. Enticing meal deals will encourage customers to spend more while they feel like you're offering a better deal.

Dig into those details and think about your business in ways your competitors have not. What level of lighting is best suited for your customer experience? What does it smell like when they walk into your establishment? Should you install a smell machine? What type of seating and decor fits your business? What styles will encourage customers or clients to give you their money?

When this is done right, your customers ask fewer questions and are positioned to buy your product or service. Do they trust you? If not, you need to run through every detail and make sure your customer experience aligns with what you're offering.

Even the banks use ambiance to bring you inside and put you at ease, so you trust them with your highly personal information. From the smells, windowed office design, friendly face-to-face greetings, and music, banks use the senses to engage trust and transparency in the lobby atmosphere. They know you won't give your Social Security number to just anyone.

Chapter 5

What Is Your Mission?

*Do not call it a mission statement. Your mission
is more than a statement; it is your way of
doing business.*

Your Mission Adjusts To The Battlefield

The mission in year one should not be the same as in year ten.
Your values will change when you mature as a company and as
a craftsman. The challenges you battle against in year ten can
seriously differ from those you started with in year one.

The best businesses adapt and evolve with internal and external
changes. Identifying a core mission of what's important to you
and why you're in business at the start lays your foundation.

Business Is War™

Your business is like a young fighter preparing for his first fight.
Your mission statement becomes your game plan—it helps you
outline your objectives, tactics, and values. The landscape of the

market shifts, bringing you new challenges and opponents. Your mission statement must evolve like your coach adjusts strategies to meet the changing dynamics of the fight. Holding onto the same mission statement without adapting it as you grow is like entering the ring with ancient weaponry. To thrive and emerge victorious, you must continuously refine and update your mission to align with your goals, market conditions, and customer expectations.

For example, imagine that your company started by making toasters but evolved into manufacturing televisions after some time. You risk throwing your business out of alignment if your mission doesn't change as your vision matures. You may have started with a mission to become the best toaster maker, but your business is out of alignment if you don't evolve your mission to become the best television maker as you switch products.

Look at Sears, AOL, Kmart, and other big-name brands that were everywhere when you grew up and are no longer available. They probably had a good mission when they started, but they didn't adapt to changes in their business and industry and couldn't survive.

Consider how COVID forced restaurants, hotels, and other businesses to evolve and change to meet safety protocols. Touchless innovations became part of the customer journey. Rooms went longer between cleanings to limit contact, and pharmacies adopted drive-throughs and curbside assistance as additional safety measures. Home deliveries increased. Many of these changes became habits that still exist today.

This goes back to Amazon's ingenuity in keeping up with its customers' wants. They're building warehouses in the middle of nowhere so they can ship products to you the same day. It's working so well that other companies are trying to play catch-up to compete with them.

Your mission has to be in style with you. It needs to be editable and able to evolve with you. It needs to be something you can really get behind in year one. It will not and should not look the same in year 20. Think about how the pre-COVID economy is different from the post-COVID economy. Your business mission statement needs to be fluid enough to evolve through changes like that.

The Mission of Bonita Payments

When I first started Bonita Payments, I just wanted to be in business because I had no choice. I could not imagine myself going to work in another corporate setting. The corporate world is full of pressure, rejection, and insecurity. One minute, they love you; the next, they hate you. I started Bonita because I saw a gap in the way they treated people in corporate America compared to the way I wanted to treat people in my business.

Private ownership became an important component of my mission as part of my need to be different from the corporate mindset. I've seen corporate America fire that older lady who has been there for over 20 years. There wasn't a good reason to fire her. Their strategy had changed, and they wanted a younger, newer image that she didn't fit into.

You've probably seen it, too. That newscaster who isn't considered pretty any longer is ditched for a younger, cheaper model. It doesn't matter if she can handle the crowd, manage things when the camera acts up, and has a ton of skill. It's all about the image. It's just the way the business world works.

I envisioned a company where people aging in sales could bring skills and experience, and we could make magic together. We could make great money together, helping one another instead of cutting each other down.

I would watch my colleagues in merchant processing get angrier, meaner, and more bitter. They would get more upset and more disrespected in this world. They would get looked over for promotions. The new prospect was younger and hotter. Or, like one time, the next woman in line got looked over six years in a row because they wanted to give it to a man until finally, they just let her go after being there for 19 years.

Every day, I watched this stuff go on. They decide they want to go in a different direction, and that's what they do. Companies like this one clean the books at the end of every year, and in the process, they drop people like hot potatoes. Something had to change, and that's why I left corporate America. I started my own company. I hired that same woman they dropped after 19 years as my first sales rep, and she's still working for me.

I wanted to do something different. When I first started, my core mission was to be an agent-focused, customer-focused, employee-driven company with a real family feel. I didn't want the pressure of a quota hanging over all of us. If you weren't hitting your numbers, you had to return to the gym to train, and we would do it together. I carried a woman that way for one year, and she's been carrying me ever since.

We don't have any miserable people in my organization. We are all winners. We train hard and pay close attention to the mission of consistent growth and evolution. No room for egos, because the battlefield keeps us sharp and on high alert. I instill my values into my teammates every day and with every encounter. It's not always easy because we are all different, but I make it DNA-level to teach and train continuously.

One thing that I am very proud of is the feelings battleground and how it applies to Bonita. I wanted to address what it felt like to work with me, and you should, too. How do people feel on the car ride to work? I wanted them blasting music and ready for the joy of being around positive people and healthy brothers and sisters in work arms. We don't want anyone listening to "you can do it" podcasts and struggling to enter our office building like it's a dreaded job.

What Changes Bonita's Mission...

My number one driver is revenue. I want the people who work for me and with me to make a perfect living, so I initially thought about survival. Now that we handle the rent, I want to see everyone reach their full potential. I want to see them be able to take their kids on vacation and do what's important to them. It makes you feel good when you know that people are working better for you financially than elsewhere. I know for a fact that we're paying more than our neighboring businesses. Our compensation-heavy and freedom-based model allows everyone to earn as much as they want, but they must deserve it.

When I look around at this, I added to my mission that we are highly paid and valued members of a team environment. I'm proud of that, but I also work to constantly refine this mission because I don't ever want to pay somebody something they don't deserve. I work hard to make them want to be contributors by pitching in and improving things. I'm constantly working on refining that to get it just right.

Your Turn: What Is Your Mission?

Take some time to build a vital mission. What is your mission? Why is that your mission? Remember, this is not a mission statement. This is a way of doing business.

I want you to dig down and define the company's culture and the reason for the company. I want you to develop a mission that aligns with your mastery, your USP, your client experience, and everything else you're building into your business. We've discussed your craftsmanship and mastery. We've defined your unique selling proposition. We've explored your customer journey. All these things will help you define your mission.

The mission statement has to be personal—you cannot have AI write your guiding mission statement.

The mission is something that you can tell the customer, the employee, or yourself that resonates with them about what it means to do business with you. This doesn't have to be perfect. Remember, it should change with your business over time, anyway.

Here's a challenge for you --->Read the mission statements for the top ten companies in the entire world. I bet you like only half of them.

Then, think of a mission statement or brand that you really like. Look at how they communicate their mission. Take notes and incorporate what you like about how they do it into yours.

In the meantime, get ready to dive deeper into the next battle in chapter six.

Chapter 6

Driving, Co-Pilot, or Passenger?

"Details matter. It's worth waiting to get it right."

~ Steve Jobs, Founder of Apple

Massive Support vs. Scalable

To create a strong business, you first need to understand the difference between a massive support company and a scalable company. Think of what you do for your clients and customers, and keep reading to determine which one your business is now.

A massive support company means the business is built around you—you're the driver. You are so good and unique as a master craftsman that the infrastructure for your company is designed to help you touch every aspect of the business with a supporting cast. You have people in place who do the ancillary tasks so you can do the specialized craftsmanship tasks.

Electricians, attorneys, dentists, CPAs, and other "masters" who use the massive support business model are examples.

These people have to build the support system needed to remain masters.

Scale refers to being able to "set it and forget it." A scalable company (where you become the passenger) is a business where you have defined your mastery in a teachable, coachable, and scalable way. You have developed the processes and protocols so that the people on your team can keep the business going and produce income even if you're not handling the product or service at that moment.

A business selling products, a technology company (software), or restaurants are typical examples of scalable businesses.

> The solopreneur is a driver—this is the business owner who just has to grind it out, doing everything on their own.
>
> In co-pilot mode, the business owner is starting to delegate and moving the business towards a state of scalability.
>
> In passenger mode, the business is scalable. You've delegated tasks out. You've got dependable automation processes in place. And you're saying, "Damn, this stuff is working. I'm floating like a butterfly."

The ultimate goal in business is to shift from a massive support company to a scalable company. This often happens when revenue increases enough to scale up your infrastructure and team.

⚠ **Warning:** This has to be done right! (I'll show you how this can go wrong soon.)

Shifting Massive Support Into Scalable

Let me give you an example of an attorney who scaled his massive support business into a scalable one. Morris Bart is one of the most successful attorneys in Louisiana history. He has been named a Super Lawyer, a Million Dollar Advocate, Gambit Weekly magazine's "Best Attorney," and received a "Leadership in Law" award from New Orleans City Business magazine.

What is he good at? He is a marketing genius. Every year, he comes out with a phenomenal catchphrase and advertises to the tune of millions of dollars a month. Not a year, a month. This guy advertises like you cannot imagine. He puts millions of dollars into advertising. He gets teams of lawyers to handle the cases that get assigned. Other people are working, and he supervises the business to the point where he doesn't have to do anything anymore.

He's learned to scale his business on a massive scale. Now, he has 15 locations across four southern states. His firm is one of the largest personal injury law firms in the United States, with over 100 attorneys, a support staff of well over 200, and an annual advertising budget of $25 million.[6]

---

[6] Morris Bart Personal Injury Lawyers New Orleans 2024 morrisbart.com, accessed 3/25/2024 <https://www.morrisbart.com/about/attorneys/morris-bart/>.

Shifting to Scalable

Morris Bart shifted from a massive support one-office firm to a scalable firm by paying attention to everything I lay out in this book. He built his processes and training systems to match the growth he envisioned.

Other massive support companies can do this, too. Hair stylists can recruit and train to expand into multiple salon locations. CPAs can serve more clients by opening more offices. Dental specialists, medical specialists, etc., broaden their businesses by scaling into more communities.

My Company's Biggest Struggle

I needed to scale my business, but it was the hardest thing in the world for me to do. Watching people do something in 30 minutes that would take me three minutes made me learn patience. I had to learn acceptance. I had to learn the business model of I do, we do, and then you do as I allowed others to learn how to do what I mastered.

That stuff was not easy for me. It's still not easy for me. Sometimes, I would rather just pull over and do it because I solve problems for a living. It's so easy for me to solve the problem versus telling somebody else to solve it. And my attitude is that if I need to tell you to solve the problem, you're not paying attention. I'm still learning patience.

So, I have struggled over time. I would say the single biggest struggle in my business has been in human resources. It has been in people because it's one of the only things you can't control. And you know what? You take it personally.

Scaling is a Battle That Takes People

One of the questions that I often ask employees is, "Are you aware that you're hurting these people's business?" If I receive bad service or rudeness at the counter, I will say something.

Most hourly employees don't even know this, and most business owners are at a disadvantage when it comes to staffing. You want to assemble the best team to help you win a championship, which rarely happens in today's labor force. I don't want to sound all doom and gloom, but you cannot improve the feelings of your business if your personnel are not on board.

To properly scale your business, you need solid people. When I began making enough money to hire good people, here's what I started doing—it's a trick I learned from a podcast. Give a basic task to somebody every day. "Hey, I need you to write this email for me and tell this person this and this." Every day, I did that, giving them a new skill. It just takes time. At the end of the year, I looked at how well they developed from doing the seemingly inconsequential tasks I required of them. Now, I have several reliable soldiers on my team.

As I look at the big picture, we've reached a decent place in scaling Bonita. I still get to support my agents because I have the most technique and tenure, but they can operate without me looking over their shoulders.

It takes patience and commitment to teach others to do what you do. You show them what to do, then we do it together, and then you do it. You have to go through this process to empower your team and build a scalable business. The more you do for your employees, the more you rob them of their self-esteem.

Chapter 11 covers human resources and how to build a team that makes your business profitable. Think about it. Would you let a nine-dollar-an-hour seasonal worker manage the feel of your million-dollar business?

> **Why do I like the idea of a passenger, AKA Scalable Business?**
>
> When I build a Scalable Business, I focus on setting clear objectives and developing long-term plans. Delegating operational tasks to a qualified team allows me to empower employees to take ownership of their responsibilities and grow. My time and mastery are leveraged more effectively. I can innovate my business in response to changing market conditions. I build a stronger work culture with better morale and output. Automating and delegating help me create a business with more sustainable growth and scalability. When I'm the driver, AKA Massive Support Company, my business cannot grow.

Do It Right! Don't Outscale Your Mastery.

Let me tell you a story about this lady who worked with me. She mastered operating a food truck business and was very popular with every customer. She touched every plate, and she took a picture with every customer. She had a knack for selling to all the hungry men with her charm and charisma. She grew her business by accepting a deal from a real estate investor to scale into physical locations.

She never had a training system built into her expansion plan—no recipes, modules, customer service, best practices, or anything else. She had only our point-of-sale system, which allowed her to link locations, reporting tools, and a few different things across our platform.

She grew to six locations in a very short time with no structure in place. You could go to her first location and get some food, but it would taste different at the second location, with different prices. Then, when you go to the third location, the food tastes completely different and doesn't even look the same. Across the six locations, the taste, appearance, and even the names were different.

It was a classic example of a business moving way too fast. It has been said a million times that fast success builds ego, and slow success builds character. She didn't have a tax strategy in place, the real estate battle mapped out, or any of the battles I will ensure you think of in this book.

This lady wanted all the social credibility of those six locations, but she didn't do the work to become a master at having physical business locations. She outgrew her mastery and could not make the jump from massive support to scalable. As a result, her businesses failed, and she blamed everyone but herself.

This is just one example of outscaling your mastery and setting your business up for failure. If you want to set your business up for success, you absolutely must level up your mastery to match the scalable nature of your evolving business.

In the next chapter, we take on your business numbers in the Battles of Business™ list. Don't skip ahead. Each one of these battles will build upon the other to help you win the war.

Chapter 7

Succeed On Purpose: It Starts With The Numbers

"If it doesn't make sense at one dollar, it doesn't make sense at one million dollars."

Setting Your Price Point

You are not allowed to take shortcuts when setting your prices. You have to understand the market, including its financial aspects. You need to look at what other businesses are charging in your space. You cannot determine if you have a good price or build a good price strategy until you effectively know what's going on in this market.

Open your eyes wide. Pay close attention to it and put yourself out there—be obsessive. Next-level business mastery means having a signature price. It's a place of respect. You have to find the sweet spot in your industry and your space that's not too cheap and not too expensive.

Wait! Why aren't we talking about costs right now? Because that's not how you win. Many business owners make the mistake of jumping to the cost first, but you must understand the price point before that!

Free has no value when it's all said and done.

Rule #1: Don't give your stuff away for free because they will never respect you if they can get it for nothing.

Rule #2: The more you discount, the more people discount your credibility.

Costs of Goods Sold (COGS)

You have to master understanding how the numbers affect your COGS. You can't play around with this. You have to master them. You'll consider all these in figuring your COGS:

- The cost of your labor.
- The cost of real estate.
- Your inventory.
- What are your total costs versus your overall revenue?

Do you understand your numbers?

Imagine you own a bar, and someone asks, "How much have you invested in one glass of Scotch?" Are you prepared to answer that question with confidence?

Maybe you don't because you only want to make a little money with your business and pay your bills. There's nothing wrong with that. I did it for years, but if you're reading this, you're ready to get serious. You want to know how much is in every little piece of your product line.

> Many startups fail because they don't control their cash flow and mismanage their revenues. If most businesses stall out because of funding, then it would make total sense to direct their growth based on incoming income. It is okay to give your business some grace, allow yourself time to grow, and keep moving with a master plan. Comparing your 5-month-old business to a 5-year-old business is insane. We all know comparison is the joy thief, so sing classics like The Greats until your songs become a smash hit!

Know your margins.

Research the margins in your industry and set your benchmark safely in the friend zone. You can only optimize for maximum profits by understanding the goal. A Google search can provide some of the averages to get you started. The last thing you want is to be the most expensive, and you certainly don't want to be the cheapest. The price point you want is called brilliant, so shoot for it.

You must prepare for every possible situation in a fight, and business is a fight for survival. Boxing is unlike business because you spend most of your time training for the big day. In business, you just dive in and learn to swim, all while taking loss after loss indefinitely. My time in corporate prepared me to a large degree for many of the pitfalls that I would encounter in business. You need to know the Cost of Goods Sold (COGS) and your operating expenses before you step into the market.

Your COGS are the weight of your gloves. This is what will determine how heavy your financial punches are going to be.

Your operating expenses are like understanding your opponent's reach. They define how far your resources will stretch.

If you disregard these metrics, you're like the boxer who steps into the ring blindfolded. You may land a few lucky shots, but you're more likely to get beat badly. You have a strategic advantage with the knowledge of your COGS and operating expenses. You'll be able to move with precision and be more prepared for whatever the market throws at you.

Master Your Operating Expenses

Let me repeat that: **Master your operating expenses.** You must have the goal and attitude to master knowing your operating expenses. I'm talking about that bar owner understanding exactly how much they paid for the glass and the ingredients in their drinks, PLUS how many pennies that one serving costs of their overall operating expenses.

Secondly, your partnerships are vital to how you survive and thrive in business. Are you buying from a wholesaler? Are you buying from a distributor? Are you dealing directly with a supplier?

Speaking of partnerships, as that bar owner, I would call every new and up-and-coming wine company or spirit company and ask them if they wanted me to distribute their product. Bypass the marked-up wholesaler that is making their margins gain off of you. If you understand retail, you can do anything. Buy Low, Sell High.

Where are you on the food chain? The more you can understand this, the more you understand how the pricing strategy needs to work on your level and maybe even what it takes to reach the next level.

Let's say you want to get to that next level. Perhaps you ask your partner, "How do I get there?" If they say, "You need to buy 1 million a year," that's the goal you're aiming for. If you're buying 500,000 right now, double your purchase power to reach the next level.

Maybe you can do it, maybe you can't. This is where your obsessive and compulsive level of understanding of your business will come into play. You'll look at what you're spending monthly, such as real estate costs, which we'll discuss in the next chapter. You'll pull up your bank account statements and look at every line, creating a list and asking each time, "What is the expense getting me, and is it what I expected?"

You need to have a level of mastery of your operation expenses.

One of the things business owners cry about is that merchant processing can be expensive. Do you know how much you are paying? Are you paying for things you aren't using? Are you getting hit with per-occurrence fees because you haven't taken the right actions?

The truth is that merchant service isn't going to be the most costly expense you have. The individual transaction fee is 100% tax deductible. In my portfolio, business owners who do the best and make the most money are the ones who don't sweat the credit card fee.

You simply include the cost of merchant fees in your price. A cup of coffee does not cost $7. You place all your operating costs and profit margin in that price handsomely.

Also, look at how much more dangerous carrying cash is than using credit cards. Credit cards come with safeguards to protect your money when they're used properly.[7]

Do you have questions about the role your merchant processing plays in building and expanding your business? Jump on the phone with us, and we'll talk you through the best payment solutions for your business. >>call or contact form?<<

---

[7] SELECT (2024, March 15). Here are 3 reasons why paying with a credit card is safer than a debit card or cash. Cnbc.com. Retrieved March 25, 2024, from https://www.cnbc.com/select/why-paying-with-credit-card-safer-than-debit-cash/

Chapter 8

The Real Estate Battleground

The interest of the landlord is always opposed to the interests of every other class in the community.
~ David Ricardo

Ignore This Now: Pay Later

Real estate is among the top three things you can do to help or hurt business, sharing the spotlight with craftsmanship and financial management. You build a business with craftsmanship mastery, anchor the business with real estate, and operate the business through finances. Skip any of these, and your business success will be in serious jeopardy!

The Landlord Matters!

Everybody has had a shitty landlord, haven't they? The shitty landlord wants their rent and doesn't want to fix absolutely anything. It is a standard to be a terrible landlord. I have always wondered why so many get into real estate to be a terrible landlord. It is unfortunate because it happens every day, all the time, everywhere.

One surefire way to kill a startup is to enter a marriage with a bad landlord.

The best businesses have the best landlord-tenant relationship, and they both bring something to the table. Look at the mall. The nicest malls that you can ever find will have the nicest tenants, and they'll both bring something to that eco space harmoniously. For instance, Saks Fifth Avenue is generally in a nice place that echoes Neiman Marcus on the other side. It's the same with Rolex, Burberry, Prada, and any of the wonderful-name places.

Park your store in a crappy strip mall where they barely cut the grass, and you're on your own. They say you shouldn't judge a book by its cover, but the outside of a business will give you a great idea of what to expect inside.

The Motivated Landlord

Motivated landlords are the best; they are the ones who give you a little bit of a ramp-up. They provide an incentive that doesn't take from your revenues, no profit sharing, or similar things.

Last week, I walked into a restaurant, and the A/C was off, making the entire place feel like a sauna. I asked the manager why the A/C wasn't on, and she said they were waiting on the landlord. This is a common situation, and it happens on a regular basis.

Every lease is negotiable, and you should read the fine print to maximize what you can do to help your business. Don't ever sign a triple-net lease unless you are McDonald's! If you want to rent, be the best renter! Because being a responsible tenant can be extremely costly if you are not careful and deliberate.

If the landlord is good, you wouldn't need a lawyer, but getting one to review contracts may be in your best interest. They'll help you avoid things like a triple-net lease, which requires you to pay all expenses, including real estate taxes, building insurance, and maintenance. If you need help understanding everything in the lease, don't sign it and get legal assistance to understand it thoroughly before you sign.

This battlefield is for the landlords, too. If you're a property owner and you are not trying to give your tenants the best chance at being successful, then take your butt to another industry. Your success is attached to your tenant's success.

Scouting Out Real Estate

Establishing a business is much like setting a trap or an ambush. You need to know where they're going to travel. What may cause them to take a detour along the way to your place? What lures them inside?

Location, location, location.

When you buy a home, the curb appeal dramatically affects whether or not you'll check it out. The same is true for your business location. What impression does the outside present when people first see it? Is the area surrounding it maintained and inviting? Does the location support the type of business you're running and the business model?

Quality of Space

If you're trying to build a brand, that brand needs to be equally yoked with your property. The location itself needs to speak to your audience the same way your business does. Imagine using a convertible Porsche 911 to haul trash. That is not reaching full potential behavior, and having a location that doesn't help your business is the same thing.

The ideal location is so crucial to the short-term success of a business, probably more than any other factor!

Take Apple stores, for example. You'll never see them in city areas where the locals are focused more on survival or in an uninhabited area. Apple Stores require a locale with a gentle, modern feel, or their customers just won't walk in the door. The brand needs to match the locale. Your business and its aesthetics are part of a comprehensive package that includes your offering, your experience, how you feel, smell, taste, act, etc.

Look for a place that is as close as possible to what you're trying to do, one that can blossom into precisely what you need it to be. Make sure you understand the additional costs of getting it ready. Can you remodel it, and do you have the capital for that? You don't want to trap yourself in too expensive real estate—that's bad real estate.

Don't Start The Meter Too Soon

I tell people all the time, don't start the meter until you are making money. Do you really need real estate now? If your business doesn't tell you that you need real estate—more real estate, better real estate, more space—then don't just listen to your head.

If you recall, I told you in chapter one how we were operating out of a Volkswagen Passat with a million in revenue before we even thought about getting an office space. You have to be willing to do that, and you have to be humble enough to do it because otherwise, you're setting yourself up for failure.

Understand The Rent Per Square Feet

There are several formulas that you can use to calculate the rent per square footage for a business with your revenues. I don't have that exact formula, but I have some ideas. This type of thing is more customized for your business, so that's for a one-to-one meeting. But the point is that it cannot be rent-heavy for low revenue. You just can't do it. I don't care how much you like the location. If you can't afford it in perpetuity, you should not be messing with it.

Final Thoughts:

My last point about real estate is that you want a space that speaks for your business and looks exactly like you need it to be the best version of your business. Let real estate be an asset and not a liability, and let your business model fit the parameters of your space—not too big, not too small, but just right!

Chapter 9

Perfecting the Sales Process

"I have never worked a day in my life without selling. If I believe in something, I sell it, and I sell it hard."

~ Estée Lauder

The Driving Force To Your Revenue

You need sales, for without sales, you have nothing. Zig Ziglar said it best when he said that nothing happens until someone sells something. Sales is the day-to-day activity that will keep your business going.

You can have the best craftsmanship in the world, and you can market your butt off, but you still have to sell it. Sales and marketing must be aligned, but sales are significant because it is the one thing that you can do over and over. It's how you continuously keep revenue coming through your business so that it survives. Business Is War™ is the mantra, surviving is the beacon, and sales is the driver.

Sales is such a powerful driver that you can have crappy craftsmanship and still survive if you can sell it. Sales can cover up some other flaws your business has because the one thing you cannot survive without is sales.

The Bad Side of Sales

Sales bring responsibility. Whatever you sell, you're obligated to deliver what they purchased. You have deadlines and follow through in facilitating what you say to them. If you tell them you're the best at something, and they write a check for that best at something, you have to deliver that.

This is why you got into business—to be able to do those things. You need to be obsessed with delivering on your promise (sale). However, make sure you can deliver and don't sell "wolf" tickets, as they were called back in the day. If you can't do it, you're selling "wolf" tickets. Don't do that. Make sure you can and do deliver what you sold.

Be Obsessed With Sales

You must possess the hunger to go out there and get those sales. Be committed and driven to getting those sales. When we talk about mastering sales in your business, you're the battle-tested general focusing your efforts on securing crucial territories. You have to prioritize sales to establish your business's future success. It's not about survival—it's about thriving. You must strategically target sales opportunities just as the skilled boxer plans every move to outmaneuver his opponent. Sales is one of the most powerful weapons you wield in the war of business.

Defining Entrepreneurship

Entrepreneurship is about identifying a need, gap, or want in the market, filling it, and setting a price for it. The DJ is an entrepreneur, but he doesn't throw the party. He had to find people in this business set to get the gigs. Wherever you are on the journey, you need to master sales. There are no shortcuts.

Forget Your Family & Friends

You cannot pay your bills on sales to family and friends. Do you think your family and friends will be enough customers for your business to survive? Wrong!

> The entrepreneur's journey is like no one else's. It can be a lonely existence. Your friends will change every 12 to 18 months because they don't grow with you. You're on an island all by yourself. You don't keep friends for long, and if you do get some friends you hang onto, you've done something real.

You have to go 50 miles from your house to be an expert.

People tend to pigeonhole you into what they remember you to be from the past. They will apply this to your future and your business. Maybe you could not sew straight as a kid, but now you're starting a new clothing line. Often, the ones closest to you can't let you grow beyond what they remember of you.

You sometimes have to leave your own backyard, grow up somewhere else, and come back as a new, refined version of yourself. Don't let the support of family and friends be the only thing that drives you. Don't let it be what validates your success. Build a business outside the family, and then incorporate them on the backside if you can.

Align Your Value Proposition

There is a value proposition that you should understand. When you don't understand the value, it doesn't transition into a close or a sale. Until the customer understands the value, they won't act or react. You can talk until you're blue in the face and still not get the response you're looking for.

You must master your craft, understand the product or service you're offering, and be able to break it down. You need to be able to explain it to them so that they see the features and the benefits. You have to meet them at their level of understanding.

Let's say you're selling television sets. You must understand what that customer is looking for in their television set—what benefits are at the top of their list. Do they want to know that it is silver and the dimensions are perfect for this purchase? Do they want to know more about its mechanics or how much it weighs? Maybe they're more concerned about how easy it is to use. You have to have something for everyone in your toolset to be able to offer this product to them and secure the sale.

Multiply Your Best Customers

One of the most intelligent things you can do as a business owner is to identify your perfect customer. That's deep-level entrepreneurship.

- Who is your perfect customer?
- What are their needs and motivations?
- What is the pricing that fits them?

When you can say, "This is what I do, this is who I do it to and for, and why," you're ready to identify your perfect customer. Seek them out and adjust what you offer to this ideal customer, and then you can squeeze it into a perfect sales cycle. Start answering those questions at a detailed length with specificity over and over in your head.

I begin to multiply this ideal customer in my head so I can reproduce this customer every day because I know exactly what I want. That brings the red car analogy to life. I wanted a red car, so I started seeing red cars everywhere. Master this, and you will gain clarity and start finding more of these customers.

You've had craftsmanship, real estate, and financing, and now you have sales. You have to be able to sell your business. When all else fails, you go out there and sell something, even if it takes knocking on some doors. Then, you align your sales with the next battlefield—marketing.

Chapter 10

Marketing: The Story You Tell About Your Business

"You cannot get anybody to do something if they're not paying attention to you."

~ Brian Carter

Marketing and Sales are Brothers In Arms

Sales and marketing are intertwined and must be aligned. Sales are tangible. I sell an item for a price. I have income and revenue from those sales. Marketing lets me tell a story and create a narrative around the sales and the product to aid the sales effort effectively.

Marketing is the true version of the story that you tell. It's a complete and total depiction of your business. You use it to tell your story and get your narrative out there. You want to be the head of the narrative. You don't want somebody else telling your story. You do not want to be at the mercy of somebody else just doing whatever. No, sir. You don't want anybody else telling your story. You tell your story.

When Marketing Goes Wrong

Bad marketing is targeting the audience you want instead of the one you have. Speak to the people who do business with you. Remember what I told you about the perfect customer and how you should target the perfect customer? Well, you can waste your marketing dollars on the wrong customer.

When you fail to create a strategic marketing plan, you can spend your advertising dollars and your marketing budget talking to somebody who would never do business with you. And that is a misappropriation of funds in every possible way.

An example of bad marketing may be that you have a neighborhood bar, but you are advertising 10 miles away from your neighborhood. Why would you have a billboard 10 miles from your neighborhood bar when everybody who comes to your bar is within walking distance?

Be A Tracker!

If you just put a message out there and sales come back, you want to know where they heard it from. Which one of the marketing vehicles drove them back into you? You must know if there is a benefit to the dollar you spend. Otherwise, it's like just operating your business with your eyes closed. Why would anybody in their right mind ever want to do that?

Be obsessive. You want to be in business, and you want to be meticulously detailed and specific about it. You want to ask your customers and clients how they heard about you. You want to know your cost-per-lead and cost-per-transaction. Go as deep into the details as possible because you need to know what works to do more of it.

Make Them Hear You

Tell your story to as many people as possible, anywhere and everywhere. The more you can do it, and the louder you can be, the better. Guerrilla marketing talks about being aggressive and being dirty in some cases. And by dirty, we mean wherever your competitors are marketing, you step right into the same room, try to overpower them, and tell the same exact story with brighter colors. It's actually vicious.

Cola Wars

Pepsi and Coca-Cola have long been going after one another in mutually-targeted marketing campaigns. Starting around five years ago, they took on a more light-hearted sparring competition on social media and in their ads. Sometimes, they make viewers laugh. Other times, they don't, but it does start a conversation every time. In this case, having fun with the marketing and stepping into one another's domain has become a win-win situation for both sides.

If you think about commercials, there are two types: the ones that inspire and the ones that answer questions. Marketing is one of those things that must align with the culture, the way you feel, and the way the brand is represented. It is essential that you tell the truth about your business because the last thing you want is for your marketing to misrepresent what you actually do.

Learn From The Best Companies

Rolex doesn't sell watches; it sells timepieces and status symbols. Its marketing is aimed at established people looking for signature items to elevate their appearance. You could tell the time on an Apple Watch or your iPhone. Everybody with an iPhone knows what time it is. But people buy Rolexes as status symbols.

If I could give marketing advice to any small business or entrepreneur, I suggest pretending that you have the single most amazing, unique, beautiful, intelligent, perfect, and satisfying product in the world and telling the story just like that. Just make sure that you can deliver it!

Let me go back to that attorney from chapter six. This attorney fills the television, billboards, and radios with advertisements about his law firm. It is his namesake. He's become synonymous with injuries, accidents, and legal problems through these catchphrases. He has so much marketing around it that people forget he's an attorney. They just know his name, but yet, whenever they think of an attorney, they think of his name. So, he's done a phenomenal job of flooding the market with enough continuous content to become a household name. And that's one way to do it. You can just constantly tell the same thing over and over and over. We all know that if something is said enough times, it becomes the truth.

Chick-fil-A has a cow on its logo, but it sells chicken. That logo incites humor and establishes a memory hook! It's an excellent example of how your logo must be part of your marketing. Your logo is a visual aid for your company. It is the billboard or signage for your company. The name on your building, the logo on your website, and everything else must be consistent. What you hear and what you say need to look alike to describe your business properly. They need to be aligned.

Chevron's biggest marketing push is its claim that it has the cleanest fuel and the cleanest bathrooms. It pushes this claim everywhere in its marketing, showing that if you say it to enough people, they will believe it 100% and tell everyone else about it.

Study what your favorite brands do and how they do it. Study how others in your industry run their marketing, then do it better.

The Customer Paradox

Every entrepreneur or business owner suffers with their customer in some way or another—whether it be too close for comfort or lack of loyalty because of market saturation.

Starbucks taught people to grab a cup of coffee from an online order and never speak to a barista. This same lesson is why customer and employee relationships are in the toilet. There was no need for a friendly smile when all the business was handled in the cloud. Today, customers are not loyal. They'll support whoever has the cheapest price or the brightest sign. Most strip malls have multiple stores selling the same things. The options are plentiful if you expand that to a one-mile radius.

I would never open a business and let Google or Yelp criticize me from the cheap seats—there is no more helpless position to take than that. Most people are not going to these apps to write beautiful blogs filled with pictures about their experiences. They are there to trash a brick-and-mortar. This is a tricky situation for any startup that is doing the best it can with the available resources. I have seen the absolute worst customers, and it looks more and more like we are breeding them daily.

The customer expectations set by the online shopping experience are often unrealistic. Perfect pictures, a seamless checkout process, and lightning-fast shipping with constant notifications. These are the standards set by the digital world.

But to err is human, and it's inevitable to encounter a few hiccups when dealing with a human in a physical store. So, expectations are always going to be skewed when it's a human versus a robot. Our society is already pitted against the hourly employee who has real-life issues visible on their face.

Between bad and spoiled customers and social media telling employees that they are underachieving, we are doomed in the realm of business to meet consumer expectations. So, what can a small business do to keep pace with the ever-changing commerce landscape?

SURVIVE!

Take back the narrative of what is to be expected when doing business with you. Use the real human senses inside your store. Create a vibe that the online can't match! The benefit of the store is the decor, the smells, the sounds, the visuals...the people!

That is how you compete with online perfection. I would much rather go to a dealership and leave with a car than buy it online. Customers are so much more likely to say yes after a test drive. The eyes are the windows to the soul!

Human Resources is one of the biggest challenges in portraying the right story to your customer. In Chapter 11, I talk more about this battle you must win.

Chapter 11

People Will Do What People Do

"A genuine leader is not a searcher for consensus
but a molder of consensus."

~ Martin Luther King Jr.

All the battlefields and pain points of starting and running a business will pale compared to the complicated waters of managing, staffing, and working with people. I have overpaid to get minimal results, I have underpaid to get better than average results, and I have yet to find the perfect tune to resonate with people for optimal results.

As a business owner, you will go through 100 employees to find the one that is right for your mission. When coaches perform tryouts for a professional basketball team, the best show up and compete at the highest level for the limited positions available. But in small business, we don't approach new team members like a draft or a tryout. Because today's labor force is not what it once was, we don't have many options. Somewhere in the last ten years, it became cool to be a YouTuber and not an Engineer. Somewhere in the last ten years, it became cool to be an Influencer and not an Attorney. Many people shy away from soft-skilled jobs, and if they do them, it leads to pitiful returns riddled with nasty attitudes.

> Customer service across all industries is in shambles, and big companies like Walmart and Amazon are looking to replace those bad attitudes with happy robots! Can you blame them?

The wage-pay conversation is so broken nowadays that the least skilled positions command higher than justifiable pay. Job values are inflated along with the dollar, and the expectation gap has never been wider. The previous generation knew they were employees and lived with honor around their jobs. But over the last ten years, the fake social media influencers have all but killed the labor force with inflated pay expectations and telling the wage earner that they are all bosses and CEOs. The cascading effect is that human capital is at an all-time low. Detroit was once known as Motor City, and getting a job in the automotive industry guaranteed you and your family a great life. They moved those operations to Mexico for cheaper labor rates and a more grateful employee base. No Union beef or business crippling insurance that makes it far too expensive to employ Americans.

I cannot describe a more complex arena than HR or Human Capital. This crapshoot makes every business owner or entrepreneur question themselves and their mission. Investing in people and wondering if the return on the investment will ever happen makes it the most expensive and nerve-racking area of proprietorship.

One of the biggest reasons HR is so nerve-racking is that 19% of Americans are reportedly late to work at least once a week, and if you terminate them for it, they're still subject to unemployment benefits.[8] You could even risk being litigated against.

Why Is HR So Complicated?

There is no more complicated space in a business than that of the human capital. It's the only thing that you don't have control of. You can control software more than you can a human. You don't know if they will show up on time because dollars don't determine timeliness. Pay scales don't determine actual effort at work.

When I learned that you couldn't pay a person enough money to be the best version of themselves, I understood that their minds are their own. You can do nothing to control, influence, or possess their actions. People will do what people do.

Back in the day, you used to go to work, and it would be a badge of honor to work at the Ford plant, General Motors plant, or any car manufacturer. People would work there for their entire lives, go home with pensions and benefits, put their kids through college, and take family vacations. Today, the same generation of children who benefited from that blue-collar plant work would consider that a loser job, but today, they also don't have a better job.

---

[8] Flynn, J. (2023, September 8). *15+ shocking late for work statistics [2023]: How often + why are Americans late for work?*. Zippia. https://www.zippia.com/advice/late-for-work-statistics/

Between social media and entrepreneur marketing, people have miscalculated what a good job is and what good employees are. People continue to overestimate their value to a business, sometimes having a toxic relationship with their employers. Dishwasher pay has steadily increased with inflation to the point that the entry-level position in hospitality has hurt restaurants' profits.

Amazon is trying to figure out how to use drones to deliver packages. If they can get away from the human component of a business, they will. That's why online ordering is so much better than picking up a phone and trying to order something from a human being. That's why the touchless car wash is better; you don't have to talk to anybody. That's why email is so much more reliable than postmail.

Hiring a Sports Player

Employees who play sports offer a different type of value. Playing sports takes dedication, a competitive spirit, and a fortitude that helps them thrive under pressure. They've learned how to be part of a team, take guidance to improve, and understand how to make goals.

What Are People Looking For In A Job?

Some people would rather work at a local coffee shop, making five dollars plus tips, than at a corporation, making $15 or $20. They are buying into a culture, an environment, and anything that doesn't look like regulated work. People want to be free-spirited.

The cubicle-style workspace may have built this country, but people look down on the cubicle today.

People aren't just looking for a job anymore. They're buying into your brand and mission. Your brand is something they can get behind. The more you do this right, which involves the things we've already discussed, the more potential long-term team members you'll attract.

I use video marketing and practice clear brand value. I put out content talking about doing better, being better, with teachings on being more aggressive, being on offense and not defense, having a take-charge attitude, and being more "now" minded. People come to join us because they like the way I represent our company.

I marketed them into our company. Through my content, they see something they want to be part of. That makes us different at Bonita from stiff, stale sales jobs. Typical sales jobs have a catch-and-kill spirit. At Bonita, we have a catch-and-grow energy.

Again, the more precise you are on your brand and mission and how you operate your business, the better people you'll attract. You can do more than just leave this to chance versus reach out with your culture and work ethic. If people are working for your competitors, ask why. Find out what you need to do differently.

Inspiring Leadership

Some of the most outstanding leadership I witnessed came during my military career, where I learned to be on time and dress better. Be organized, keep a clean shave, and don't show up to work smelling like the good time from the night before. One of my close friends has a saying: If you stay ready, you don't have to get ready. This simple philosophy will keep you available for an opportunity should it arrive.

Good leaders set clear boundaries and reward team members who respect the company, themselves, and each other. People want to be part of something greater than themselves and to feel appreciated. It's not always money they're after. Sometimes, it's acknowledgment. Set a culture that includes holiday parties and employee benefits like meals and gift card programs for jobs well done. You need things to make your employees proud of being the best at their jobs; offer more than anniversary ink pens or fake watches. Leadership should celebrate milestones, every benchmark should be blown up, and every birthday should be acknowledged. If you establish a winning culture, winning will be in your company's DNA.

What Is Your Staff Doing?

Ages ago, I once pushed shopping carts at Walmart. I showed up every day on time wearing my best outfit, motivated and fully ready to go. I was 17 years old and always had that work ethic.

Today, many people show up for work and spend more time on social media on the clock than they do off the clock. Social media is addictive, and customer service is in the dumps because we are not communicating with each other. What if all companies placed a hard stop on all phone use while on the clock? I guarantee that productivity will skyrocket and profits will soar!

When making you a drink, the bartender asks you how you're doing, and they have a small conversation. You can chat about any number of things. They can do that several times a day, and that's communication. That's why you go to a bar sometimes.

This younger generation today offers very little communication, and as a result, we are all strangers. That's when I say, "Are you aware that you're hurting these people's business?" You can't go to the Apple store with an attitude. You can't work at Chick-fil-A and have an attitude. How will you make money in tips if you have an attitude? How are you unaware that a customer is ready for their check because you're on your phone? How are you not aware that somebody just walked in, and they're standing in front of you, and you're on your phone?

If you're on your phone, ignoring them while their hand is up for service, that's hurting somebody's business. People just don't realize that.

I'm picking on hospitality because hospitality is supposed to be hospitable, and that's a soft-skill job. Do you know why? Because all they're doing is following instructions and providing the service the whole time. It's not like you're moving furniture, running electrical wires, or even plumbing or something like that. We're talking about how hospitality is often no longer hospitable.

Your Team Is Your Army

If you approach your team building like a draft and a head coach, you can see the individual value each player offers and how they all work together in a team environment. This lens gives you the understanding that each player is transitional and replaceable. Your job is to galvanize a championship team and ensure that you make the playoffs every year. Your team should reflect your brand and core values, and like a fraternity, every member has to know the theme song.

Chapter 12

Taxes: Shifting Your W-2 Mindset To A Business Mindset

"The hardest thing in the world to understand is the income tax."

~ Albert Einstein

Taxes Are The Bill of Being in Business

Taxes can hurt you early, or they can hurt you late, but you will have to deal with them. You will need to master taxes to survive in entrepreneurialism. If you were a W-2 employee before starting your business, you have to shift your tax mindset.

Taxes are the bill that is never going away—a responsibility every business will have. If you are making money, then you are paying taxes. There is no shortcut, no secret sauce trick, or anything. You're going to either pay the taxes or pay the fines. You must shift from the avoidance mindset to the acceptance mindset when it comes to taxes for optimum business survival with the least amount of stress.

A skilled CPA is your trustworthy lieutenant. In navigating your taxes, your CPA will bring a high level of expertise, diligence, and strategic thinking to ensure your taxes are compliant. No way in the world can you build a business, sustain it, and grow it without a competent partner in this particular area of war.

A Great Tax Strategy Strengthens Your Business

Not only will a great tax strategy help you save costs, but it will also boost the health of your operation. Paying early will always give you a discount compared to paying late. The sooner you build it into your financial schematics, the better off you will be in the long haul.

Your business is like a fighter in training camp, and your tax strategy is your gameplan for the next opponent. Adopting a tax strategy early on will help you tighten your defenses against an older veteran that's not going away. Avoiding taxes places a weak spot in your defense where a journeyman can make the fight ugly. Your business is left vulnerable to fines, penalties, and maybe even legal battles. When you pay taxes early, you sharpen your skills. Maybe it requires more resources up front, but it safeguards your business's credibility in the ring. A sound tax strategy will help you navigate the rocky terrain of the market, helping you thrive.

Don't Mess This Up

Pay your taxes. Don't get behind, as getting behind is the death sentence in taxes. Get used to the fact that you'll probably always owe taxes because it's done retroactively. Establishing a routine with your CPA and paying your taxes as outlined for your business will save you a lot of anxiety and headaches. Avoiding taxes by putting them off is never the answer.

Understand your sales taxes and that every transaction has a sales tax. Get comfortable with the fact that this is the bill for being in business. Shift your mindset to accept all the required business taxes and turn them into a tool that helps your business succeed instead of allowing them to damage your emotional and financial health.

The final mindset shift that I needed to make to ensure my success was an understanding that the more money you make, the more taxes you should pay, and the more tax breaks you can qualify for. Criminals don't pay taxes, but true business minds use the tax code like a jab in the later rounds of a championship fight—skillfully and willfully.

Chapter 13

Money Is A Tool You Must Master

"Beware of little expenses; a small leak
will sink a great ship."
~ Benjamin Franklin

Conquer Your Fears About Money

It took me years to understand that money is a product, just like the chicken fried in the kitchen or the drink poured at a bar. Everything has costs, some more than others. Once I started mastering my cash flow, I better understood how to use my money as a tool to help me grow my business. Most of us do this naturally by choosing to pay the light bill instead of the car note because one has a much louder deadline.

We are naturally programmed to fear money because our consumer-based value system treats it as the prize. But in my understanding, money is the tool that helps you build more systems and products that earn you more money. I have been guilty of having a toxic relationship with money, and because of that, it took me far too long to place money exactly where it belongs—in my toolbox.

As consumers, we are taught to earn and spend. Very few understand how to earn and invest. The biggest problem I have with traditional teachings about money is that we are not given great opportunities to gain more wealth. Instead, we are given far more opportunities to spend our cash.

Capital Determines Your Livelihood

The amount of capital you have determines your business's health. Access to capital means that you or your business is worth the investment, regardless of the borrowing cost. There are only two ways to get money: you can earn it or borrow it. I talk about capital this way because earning it is much more organic, whereas borrowing it is much more storytelling and deserving and layered on other factors.

When you look at capital and the loan ratio to it (how expensive it is), it's about the same as if you had done it yourself and put all of your resources into it. They parallel themselves by time vs effort and energy vs access.

Do You Have Sufficient Capital?

A business with access to capital will grow faster because money can solve many problems. If you can master the interest and cost penalty of borrowing money and bury it into the initiative, then you can learn to maneuver money as you would anything else.

For instance, a retail product has a cost, and capital has a cost. If your product cost is $100k and your capital cost is $100k, you should treat them the same because they're just assets in a business. It took me years to get to the point where I would borrow $100,000 and concentrate on the $30,000 interest. How quickly did I have to pay it back? What could I use the Capital for, and where would it give the highest return?

Not long ago, I spoke with a small business owner about a project he had coming up. He was looking for some creative financing or capital investment. I said, "If you can't get it now, then you should reschedule the discussion. Push it back 90 days. Really get situated and better prepared for the opportunity, and then you'll have better options."

He said that was some great advice and that it took a lot of pressure off of him. Simply put, stress and anxiety about getting something done now with deadlines is never good for anybody. So, keep hustling. Get your finances in order. Take care of your paperwork. Make sure your credit and your bank account are intact—get all of the things you need to make this work on your side so that you're ready when that creative financing opportunity becomes available.

Anyone can want a deal, but you have to ensure that you're suitable for it and that it is right for you. When dealing with money, always make the most intelligent and safest decision possible.

Make sure you understand your total responsibility when borrowing money because it's a big responsibility. You must be able to justify the money you borrow and handle the cash flow from having to pay it back. The better you look on paper, the better you sound, the better you feel, the better your marketing, and the more likely someone will want to give you access to working capital.

Finding Capital

You have to research places where you can get money and find out who likes your business model enough to invest in you. Investors need to feel comfortable that they'll get the return on their investment and that they'll be able to get it paid back because you deserve the capital. Let me do you a favor: if you don't deserve the money, don't even ask. It is disrespectful to the lender, your business, and yourself if you ask for something you do not deserve.

The better your story, the less you have to explain it. Treat capital like an instrument you must bury into your business to use it like fuel. The best advice I can give you around money is to develop a catch-and-utilize mindset because hoarding money will only lead to poor returns and obstructed cash flow. I attempt to use every dollar I have to grow my brand and business. In the past, I would say that savers are suckers, but now I understand that savers are scary. If your money is not working for you, you are working to keep it safe. This is not a growth-based mindset, and it does not return well in growing a business.

Keep pushing. Because if you don't do it, who will?

Chapter 14

Be Unbalanced

"Let me tell you the secret that has led me to my goals: my strength lies solely in my tenacity."

~ Louis Pasteur

Be Obsessed

You will obsess over every little detail of your business and achieve mastery on every level. Your mindset will be obsessive, compulsive, disordered, and maybe a bit unbalanced. You'll have the mindset of abundance and moving forward.

Remember, nobody will believe in you if you don't believe in yourself—not even close.

Be Unbalanced

The balance that matters is your checking and savings account balance. So many people out there are talking about the four-hour work week. Successful business owners know better!

Here's something you should consider: If all you've done with your life is love your family, then ask your family if you have reached your full potential. I have people I love dearly in my life, but I would rather see them live in their purpose and reach as far as possible. I am willing to be the sacrifice so they can achieve as much as they can. Do you have people with that level of love for you?

If you don't fight harder and pull more than everyone else, your business will not survive. Human capital will not do it for you, and financial capital will not do it for you.

Make Them Believe In You

Every great company has had that one founder—that one person who just beat the clock every day to try to keep the vision alive. Every company has that one person, who committed their life to the business and maybe never got their flowers. You have to ask yourself if you're that person for your company. You are? Good! You need a protective mindset. Protect your company. Love your company. Invest everything you have into your company. Understand that it can be done. Convince anybody who will listen and tell your story to everyone who will listen. Treat your company like it's the absolute best thing that you've ever been around. And then make it so. Manifest it.

When I started, we were successful on day one. By successful, I mean we had a head start because I had nine years in a corporation doing the same thing, and I had access to the same market. If I knew back then what I know now, my company would be four to five times bigger. Instead of $10 million a year, we'd be doing $100 million a year.

I just wanted to concentrate on building it one brick at a time. I could have bought a company vehicle on day one, rented an office on day one, or hired people on day one. I just didn't do it that way. I had a mindset that said, "Pay the rent, pay the bills. One apple at a time, not more than you can chew." I built it one brick at a time using the pyramid model. I was focused and committed to doing it right with respect for myself and the mission that I anchored throughout the DNA of my company.

Adopt The Crazy Mindset

Now that I know more, I see other sales organizations doing things more aggressively than I'm doing. Let me tell you how. They have the benefit of belief on their side. Imagine what you would do if you knew you were not going to fail. Just think about that. What would you do? As much as we've accomplished, I've always acted like failure was always around the corner. This is the boxer mindset that keeps me sharp. Success requires a daily rent payment, and I keep a pocket full of money.

You have to believe you're not going to lose. You have to have a mindset of abundance. You have to read everything you can get your hands on—everything. You should know everybody's story, and what their advantages and disadvantages are. You must be an expert in every discipline in every direction around your business. That is the only way it is going to work. I have seen so many businesses succumb to comfort and celebration that the very next season would be their last.

The Balance Equation

You can be obsessed and totally locked into your business without being an asshole. In my time watching and supporting entrepreneurs and learning from founders and great business minds, I've seen more than enough leaders to know how they all start and finish the race. In academics, a 50% on a test of 100 is a failure, and that is what it sounds like when I hear people talking about balance. It takes every single blood cell in your body to fight against the enormous odds facing your business.

If you constantly watch the time clock and thank God for Friday, then you are already living for the weekend and missing all the week that you should be doing your best to grow your business. Most people today do not work an 8-hour day, and if they do, there is an excellent chance they could be more productive during that time.

The type of commitment I am looking for is simple but not easy. Separate your business from the businesses operating in your market by being the difference and making the donuts. So many founders create something incredible only to pass the baton to a privileged next generation of softies that will all but kill the dream. Do the work, put in the reps, and pay attention to the details. We live in a time when people seek comfort and don't even want to pay for it. I am asking for a religious level of commitment to your business as if your salvation depends on it.

If you have to pull from desperation or obsession, maybe even hyper compulsion, to do the damn thang, then use that. You will never be able to achieve greatness without great and unbelievable work. It drives me crazy to see small business owners using their company revenues to paint a false social media narrative that contradicts their real lives. I once knew the founder of a tech company that lived in his office and didn't have a car. He basically wore the same clothes every day and gave up dating for a time. Five years later, his idea sold for high eight figures, and he still sits on the board of his company, but he got his idea to the Nasdaq.

Take your idea public, do the work, and stay laser-focused on reaching your full potential. You only have so many good years of youthful energy, why not use that time to paint a masterpiece?

Chapter 15

It's Someone Else's Life You're Living Until You Choose To Live Your Own

"May your choices reflect your hopes, not your fears."
~ Nelson Mandela

You Have Two Paths In Front Of You

Do nothing or take action!

If You Choose To Do Nothing

Nothing is going to happen until you're ready. The graveyard is full of regrets, and the life you want is a few hard decisions away. If you genuinely use the battle tools and work your butt off to put the time in, you can get there. You just have to be willing to almost be angry. You have to use whatever emotion it is. Remember, I said I've described it before as an obsessive level—compulsive level. For me, that's what gets me over the hump because I got that.

I have a compulsive level of obsession that'll get me through it. Oh, I'm tired. You can't be obsessive, and you're tired. You can't be compulsive, and you're tired. So you have to use whatever emotion you can to get yourself unstuck. You have to do something. I can't pull a person kicking and screaming to a better life. You have to do that for yourself. If you're a business owner or a potential business owner and you've read my book and you are not ready to take action, then you have to make peace with the fact that this is not the journey for you. It's just not. It's unfortunate, but it's just not. You have to make peace with that.

If You're Ready To Take Action

Congratulations. You've decided to become a better business owner and prepare yourself for the inevitable war ahead. I recommend you take the ammunition given, utilize it, and intelligently approach every day like a survival-or-die situation.

You've made the decision. Use our tools. Join our network. Become a part of our Army where every Soldier can become a General. I'm excited that you've chosen to become elite. These are the people who stop talking about it and do something. In all honesty, deciding to become a better business owner and an entrepreneur and putting yourself out there is the first step. If corporate America doesn't fit you and traditional trade doesn't fit you, then you find yourself and anchor yourself into entrepreneurship.

They're going to call you crazy at first, but then they're going to ask you for a job later when you make it work. We have all seen this movie a million times.

Winning Against Failure

What does business failure look like? Can you live in the same city as your once-open business? Do you have to terminate an employee who was a good employee because you can't make the payroll? Do you have to tell your landlord that you can't pay the rent and you risk losing your deposit? Will you lose all the furniture that you have in your place because the door locks have been changed? Even after your business fails, you still must deal with the IRS, which is looking for an annual settlement from your time in business. That's right, you still must pay taxes on a failed business. Any number of negative legal issues can arise after a failed old college try.

Plenty of suffering comes from succumbing to the Battles of Business™. Everything you did to get your idea into this world goes away when you wave the white flag. Failure is not final, but it doesn't feel good, and it destroys your credibility when you have eight startups and zero businesses that have lasted longer than 24 months.

If you take your time and measure before you cut, you can insulate your business from all the slings and arrows that await you at every turn. Business is War™ is a strategy designed to use intelligence and feel to help you win. Anyone who has ever been in a fight knows how serious it is. We know how much your defense keeps you alive and how much your offense scores the points to win the battle. So when you step into the ring, wear your name on your trunks and ensure that your robe bears the name that you are willing to fight for.

Conclusion

The Battles of Business™ we've covered in this book are:

1. Perfecting Your Craft
2. The Feelings Your Business Produces
3. Your Mission
4. Developing Scalability
5. Mastering The Numbers
6. Choosing Your Real Estate
7. Your Sales Strategy
8. Marketing Strategy
9. Human Capital
10. Maintaining Taxes
11. Financial Capital
12. The Right Mindset

That's 12 fights that you can step into the ring and be able to win that you may not have known about before you picked up this book. The possibility of achieving success and reaching further as a business owner is in your hands now that you understand what these battles entail.

You understand more about business than before and have adopted a healthier mindset. You're obsessed with getting every detail right and knowing every angle of running your business.

You understand that everything in business comes with a cost, and you've adopted a savvy mindset that considers the return on proceeds from utilizing those costs the right way. You understand that money is a tool to use strategically to level up and bring in a sound return or recurring income.

You now understand the value of intelligent, caring, generous, savvy, prepared, and open-minded leadership. You grasp how developing this leadership will also create a productive, energized team that brings in more sales.

Mastering the next level has become your beacon call to action. You're ready to train to step into that ring and win every fight leading to your business success. Most small businesses are so set on fixing their money problems that they will never get a chance to address the subliminal message that their company produces.

Not you. You know how things connect with the consumer on a deeper level: the branding on the hamburger packaging, the giant lighting over the jewelry case, the use of the black tablecloth instead of white, the background music in the restaurant, the popcorn smell at the movie theater, and the friendly chatbot at the bottom of every single shopping website.

You can do so many things to distinguish your business from the many in the market who are directly or indirectly competing with you. I challenge you to take what you learned from this book and sit down to look at your front door and feel what it feels like to do business with you.

What if you built a team full of smiling faces to greet your customers and make them feel like champions? Imagine how you could win more customers who are currently shopping on lifeless, although beautiful, websites to buy the same products you sell. How would that strengthen your revenue stream by doing your job and supporting them throughout the process, leaving no question unanswered or opportunity unaddressed?

Do nothing and nothing changes. If you're lucky, your business will continue to survive but will not reach a thriving level in this business landscape. Forget establishing a business that will survive another pandemic. Forget fortifying your business with the tools that allow it to compete with the more prominent companies and still grow and thrive. Get used to feeling worn out because you cannot delegate duties to others and have no automation in place that allows you to scale your business.

If you're still here, I doubt that's you. I bet you're ready to master success. Like the Asian Bistro client I helped turn one location into five and grow revenue from $50K per month to $1 million per month.

I can show you how to win the championship fight in the Battles Of Business™ through our Business Is War™ bootcamp series. Visit www.businessiswar.net to sign up for the Bootcamp. Start living your life on purpose. DING DING: It's Round One!

About the Author

Elliott Forman, once a force in the ring, now wields his entrepreneurial spirit as the founder of Bonita Payments, blazing trails since 2014. Beyond business, he's a maestro on the golf course, fueled by the roar of supercars and the pump of intense workouts. When not strategizing over espresso in a corner cafe, he's lost in the pages of a book or orchestrating his next move. Rooted in the vibrant pulse of New Orleans, Elliott resides with his loved ones, forever crafting his legacy.

www.ingramcontent.com/pod-product-compliance
Lightning Source LLC
Chambersburg PA
CBHW070939210326
41520CB00021B/6963